Poems

from The Bubble of Now

Andrew MacLaren-Scott

Just some poems, as they came

Prologue

The lamp of the sun was ninety-three million miles behind me and throwing out the light on its eight minute journey to skim past our planet, only for a little bit of it to be denied the freedom of a long and lasting sprint through space by hitting the moon and bouncing back and down and through my frosted window and into my eye, where - bump - it was captured, absorbed, its journey done so soon.

Where, I wondered, would this captured light's near-neighbor rays that just made it past the moon end their longer journeys? In some other and very strange eyes, perhaps, that will one day be looking up at the stars and wondering if anybody else is, or ever was, out there?

The moment in which such thoughts reside never starts or ends, but is the place where we live, always trapped in The Bubble of Now as things flow into it and things flow out. And here, as always, that moment is with me. The mysterious moment, that swaps and switches and changes, somehow.

Onward, it changes
but always the same, somehow
for always it stays
as The Bubble of Now.

Move over, move on

Don't be defined by what you used to be
and the disappointment of what you are not
nor constrained by where you wanted to go
but move on now from what you have got
The choices you made could be wrong
the path that was travelled not right
but move over, move elsewhere, move on
if a path looks inviting, tonight
The old you can still be abandoned
or some bits be retained, some forgot
The person your history suggests that you are
could well be the person you're not
Today and tomorrow, tomorrow
is all that need bother you now
Take the reins of the way you are thinking
and divert it from bad thoughts, somehow

The Bubble of Now

Trying to live life

in the bubble of now

cut off from the past

and the future somehow

living what is

not what has been

nor fearing things coming

that cannot be seen

Outside of the bubble

find worry, regret

Safe in the bubble

is the best we can get

Delightfully Dismal

It's pouring rain
I've got a cold
With every moment
I'm growing old
The Earth is held
by grim gravity
which deems Spring can't come
until the first Spring day
Things could be better
Things could be worse
Look out and smile?
Look in and curse?
My brain says 'dammit'
My mind says 'be happy'
This is our planet
and most other ones are crappy

Necessary logic

A hand raised in greeting
then slowly retracted
A shared contemplation...
then gladly distracted
No gain without pain
No life without death
No space for renewal
without constant removal
That necessary logic
is a tough thing to see
when I look in his eyes
and his eyes look at me
But his eyes are a mirror
and seeing them shine
I examine his future
and also see mine

A metaphorical moment

You may declare

that I was only watching football

and having a drink

but it was, I swear

a metaphorical moment

I think

This game

This life

This struggle

This strife

This happy

This sad

This good

This bad

Sunshine on old stone

Something about the warm glow
of sunshine on old stone
Just something about it
like there is about so many simple things
and in this cold north winter land
almost always what the sunshine brings

Digital reality

Something and nothing
is all that you need
one and zero
down a USB lead

Absence

Sometimes most important
is the thing that's not there
in the significant pause
or the space on the chair
the gap in the atoms
the sentence not said
the chemical patterns
of a mind that's now dead

Sometimes

Sometimes a man
just has to sit and wait
as time congeals
into a semi-solid state
and shoes are picked
then replaced again
and the faint tick of a clock
strikes his head with pain
The shoes go on
the shoes come off
voices become murmurs
that seem so far off
In a desperate moment
of sad introspection
he looks at a mirror
and captures his reflection
Then eventually her voice
makes him prick up his ears

but, 'I'll just try next door'

brings the man close to tears

Gas mask

In my grandmother's attic
aged about five
I found a gas mask
and lifting it to my face
I knew what it was
as I inhaled the smell of rubber
and of fear
and I wondered what it would be like
to hear
the sirens sounding
or the whistle warning
and alone in that attic
I first grasped the reality
that I would die
and as I cast the mask aside
and wandered out and back
to a sunny summer
and a searching mother

I was changed

and deranged

from the innocence of the child

as a warm quiet day

became internally cold and wild

Chemical assistance

Diphenhydramine hydrochloride
has become a new friend
to keep by my bedside
When the mind's full of madness
or thoughts bordering on badness
I can reach for the pill
that makes neurons fall still
It beats being boozy
brings on peaceful snoozy
but take it too much
and my thoughts become woozy
And I have some suspicions
when pondering amorous missions
some are dropped in my water
before I cause too much bother

Tunneled

One tunnel just leads to another
it seems to me these days
and are they harboring danger
or shelter in gloomy ways?
And that light I see at the end
is it trouble or is it my friend?
From tunnel, to tunnel, to tunnel
until the tunnel at the final bend

Keyboard

Pressing these keys
in just the right order
can make meaningful thoughts
from potential disorder
can make people laugh
or make people cry
and want to live longer
or just want to die
can make money aplenty
and the firmest of friends
or spark bitter battles
when a sequence offends
so where next I wonder
with my flickering digits
words that will help me
or meaningless fidgets?

Wondering

Forward or back?

I wonder?

Have I really any choice?

I wonder?

Any choice to wander

or not to wander

I wonder?

Today's I

My age today
is the only age I will ever be
for today is the only day
that the I of today will ever see
Each day is a life
and each evening I die
it's hard to remember
but I really must try

The morning battle

The voice in my head

said

get out of bed

The syrupy mind

in a bind

the will couldn't find

Get up

Can't be bothered

Get up

What for?

To live

Why?

You'd rather die?

Sigh...

The mental cogs clashed

and crashed

and ground

until at last

I rose

and found

improvement

until tomorrow

comes round

and

The voice in my head

said

get out of bed

The syrupy mind

in a bind

the will couldn't find

Get up

Can't be bothered

Get up

What for?

To live

Why?

You'd rather die?

Sigh...

Fighting age

Fighting bad memories
and thoughts of the future
trying to bind sanity
with thin mental sutures
It's the battle of ageing
the struggle for the old
worrying about rust
but still hoping for gold

The Badness

Waking up
feeling bad
full of every problem
I've ever had
Looking forward
feeling dread
of the journey on
until I'm dead
Looking for positives
finding none...
but then a glimmer
of an internal sun
Sit up.
Feel better
drain away
Cope and handle
just this day
Do I need a doctor?

Do I need a pill?
Or can I get better
with my own will?
I hate this badness
I hate this mad
This waking up
and feeling sad

It passes

When depression comes
remember it goes
it's here and gone
in ebbs and flows
You feel so awful
it's hard to remember
that a miserable August
could bring a happy September
Or a desperate morning
can be gone by the night
A struggle to get up
then soon feeling alright

Change the Day

I am prone to bouts of gloom
indeed deep depression
that falls over me
like a thick sticky blanket of hopelessness
and yet inside of me there is a little voice
that tries to persuade that if I could only try
I could change the day
and bit by bit cut the bastard blanket away
which is what I think I did, eventually, today
with slimy ribbons still sticking to my head
as I run away
And as for tomorrow?
Who can say?

Antidepression

Antidepression is about controlling your thinking
Turning off negatives
that can fast have you sinking
Focusing on positives
about only the day
Living the now
is the simple safe way
Good memories are welcome
the bad ones can rot
Live for the moment
with tight rein on each thought

What if?

What if this is all there is
What if this is 'it'?
No hidden mysteries
or extra dimensions
Just us, alone... Oh shit!
No parallel universes
or Gods or aliens
rocks are just rocks
with no mysterious matters
and life short and meaningless
and just for a bit?
Dead, alive, dead again
nothing then something
with comings and goings
that mean nothing at all?
It's something to think of
a point for our focus
that wet Wednesdays and boredom

are about the sum of it all

A life is an imaginary concept

When reviewing a life becomes daunting
remember it's never about your whole life
It's about living the next few minutes
to find fun and avoid pain or strife
Yesterdays and all your tomorrows...
Don't dream of reviewing that way
Why be swamped by imagined totality?
when 'your life' doesn't exist
I'd say

Living the day

My life began this morning
for I refuse to accept 'getting old'
Each day is a new beginning
A life with one day to unfold
Then I die yet again in my sleep
as consciousness dissipates and ends
to be reborn to a new life tomorrow
for whatever that new life then sends

Insomaniacal

Awake until 5 am
Lying with mind turning
wondering when
the neurons will rest
and a fevered brain
will sleep again
But awake, awake
until 5 am...
Then gone quite sudden
to return at 8
Not enough sleep
so back off again until late
Then trying to get up
as the head fills with madness
Trying to get up
to drain off the sadness
Awake, awake
trying to say

'get up, get up'
and live the day

Same thought, different day

Thinking about the future?
Remember the man said 'that's mad'
Anything beyond this here minute
is the place where the thoughts make you sad
This tea
this moment
this night
Stay in it
and you may be alright

Me on Meaning

What does it all mean?
I was asked early today
My answer is nothing
I heard myself say
Things proceeded without you
before you were here
and will march on relentless
after all you hold dear
I am dying this evening
in the moment called sleep
and dying for good
is just sleep but more deep
If it happens tonight
do you think it will matter?
The wind will still blow
and the rain will still patter
A meaningless cycle
without any deep reason

spinning and spinning

through season and season

While some talk of God

I just find that odd

Big beings there may be

but they won't care about me

Maybe I'm stupid

Maybe I'm wrong

But I won't have to ponder

these issues much longer

A tide is approaching

that will wash us away

try to enjoy its encroaching

and live for the day

The human condition

Oh… Just there…

these past few moments…

my mind was calm

and focused on now

The past was gone

the future was absent

as both are always

but that's hard to remember somehow

That girl is young

That man is old

That book is open

Its lie is sold

I have a suspicion

as I ponder submission

that frail mental chemistry

is the human condition

Mind Me

I am a Mind

So search within me

What will you find?

What will your science see?

Chemistry, moving, making thinking?

or mystery leaving science just sinking?

Atoms, molecules, ions, all matter

swirling around in nerves that chatter?

A place for freedom?

Some scope for chance?

Or a fine but predetermined dance?

A soul?

A hole...

with nothing in it?

A persisting essence?

Or something made just minute by minute?

Every day

Every day
in recent time
I wake
and feel just fine
Then as I lie
I remember, and I worry...
I have to try
not to recall
at all
or just not to lie
Sigh...

Infernal Internal

It doesn't last

remember that

it doesn't last

Well good

but that's the problem

What?

It doesn't last

Ah yes, I see

but the problem will pass

trust me

I do

but then another one will come

or perhaps another few

I know

So?

Just hang on, hang on

this one and that one will just go too

everything is so soon in the past

don't you know?

I do

So?

That's the problem, see?

What? Things lasting but things passing?

Yes, I know, there's just no pleasing me

Ah, I see

And you are?

Eh… You…

Well… Me

Armistice... Fight on...

The 12th day of November 1918
was not what some might allude
as humans fighting humans
actually just continued
and carried on, and on
with some war waging every dawn
Wars are always with us
never gone
And at the going down of the sun
and in the morning
we still fight on

Head Ahead

I am living in the dead times
I sometimes think
the empty in the head times
in black mood sink
with proper living done and gone
standing after end of song
A song that even when sung fully
was never really singing, truly
So looking back to wasted land
then gazing on at paths in sand
lifting feet, lifting head
another song
or quietly dead?
Turn...
sidestep...
a different way?
A place to sing
another day?

So now, my man

what is the plan?

The plan is yes…

is yes, you can

Writing Rubbish

Writing rubbish
keeps me sane
I've ever been thus
and will never chan…
ge
Poetry, prose
or mixed mush in the middle
If a rhyme is needed
it can always be fiddle…
d
Maybe I'm crazy
maybe I'm mad
maybe just dreadful
maybe just bad
But cheerful
not tearful
is a good way to be
and writing this rubbish

keeps cheerful in me

However…

I may think better of this

and delete in the morning

that's not a promise

it's just a clear warning

One thing about writing

is don't trust the night

never submit until looked at in light

But rubbish

gets published

That's easy to see

So if others write rubbish

then why not me?

Enough

Spaceship Earth?
A ship of fools
Fools of opinion
from nonsensical schools
What rubbish they speak
What mad belief
What blindness to ignorance
What delusions they seek
No point discussing
or writing or reading
as they anti-evolve
with intelligence receding
I'm done, I'm gone, I've had some fun
I'll find somewhere better
around some other sun

The Torturer

'I torture myself with my mind,' he said to me
as we sat together, waiting
'Oh, but you are your mind, aren't you?' I asked
'Oh! You feel that too?
Well yes, it's true
I torture myself by thinking then.'
'Which is what minds do.'
'And who are you? I don't know you.'
'Neither do I, really,' I smiled
And he said, 'Sly… That's you,'
and he smiled too
And the clock ticked on above his head
while he continued with
'My pills don't work, I think.'
'Ah, pills to stop you thinking, might be the best.'
'My mind just needs a rest,' he told me
Then his name was called
and I wished him all the best

and pondered what had brought me there

and thought, 'just cuts and bruises

damaged swollen flesh

is much better than a damaged mind

that's desperate for rest.'

Unity

I may be you

and you may be me

if our consciousness rises

from the same consciousness sea

and every half aware creature

from dog and cat to platypus

has a mind arising from the same deep thing

as you and me and all of us

your individuality an illusion

like a photon from electric waves

a temporary protrusion

that enlightens

but never stays

So be good to me

and I'll be good to you

because we are the same deep person

held in the same sticky conscious glue

Humility

The galaxies are moving outward
it seems
but anything more is guessing
almost dreams
of origins and endings
or in and out eternal wendings
Life has lived a very long time
the fossil record tells us
but tales of origins
and tales of ends
are thinkings too adventurous
We are burning fuels
like wanton fools
and pumping out dioxide
but nobody knows
if our activities pose
a genuine threat of suicide
There may be gods

there may be none

and nothing new beyond our sun

We try to reason

and draw conclusions

but false certainties

are our mad delusions

The Dark Tide

Purpose or purposelessness?
Point or no point at all?
Thoughts that allow appreciation
of why religions were invented
even with chance of truth so small
Blinking in the glare of reality
which really, surely does not care
Having the courage to face inevitability
accepting…
there's probably nothing for us there
Whether true or false
the fight continues with this thinking
that interrupts
the daily routine
and leaves the spirits sinking
A cup of coffee
time out for a rest
recalibration

forgetting future and past

just for a while, is best

Then a stubborn smile

a small rekindling of satisfaction

with an invented reason to move on

chasing some illusion

trying to ignore it's just distraction

A frail Venice of some contentedness

now glinting in sudden surprising sun

while still creaking on its sodden shaky stilts

as the dark tide recedes again

and you return to things you still want done

My father in me

When I reached an age
that I could remember my father at
everything changed
and from then on I had to measure my life
against that of him...
Am I really the same age
as when my father did this?
Am I really the same age
as when my father did that?
Am I really the same age
as when my father began to look old?
And so, soon to come, when senility took hold?
And each day in the mirror
there he is looking at me
and am I ever so slightly stooping now
as did he?

Stress

'He's off with stress, for two months now.'

'Off with stress?' the man returns

'I'll tell you what stress is...

Stress is standing in a sodden trench, aged 19

and waiting for a whistle's blow

to send you running towards raging guns.'

'Hmm... well yes,' the other one responds

'but stress is in the head

and in the head

in the mind, sometimes

just moving on, though doing nothing

can be as bad as running into being dead.'

'Nonsense.'

'Not.'

'It's nonsense.'

'It's not.'

'We disagree'

'We do

and I only hope that one day

stress in the mind does not visit you.'

'Aw stress… Boo hoo…

He needs to pull himself together man

and you do too.'

'Maybe yes… Maybe no…

Unless you are inside his head

how can you know?'

Tempus non fugit

Time flies?

Where do the years go?

Is it running faster?

Ach no…

Time is always stuck stopped

at the moment of Now

while things move into Now

and out of Now

somehow

If they didn't

forever come and go

Now would be very boring

you know

Moving on

Appreciate the pleasure
we can find amid decay
since we pass our prime
in physical life rather early
Our mind spends a long time
in a beaten-up old machine
but if that still moves and still steers
we can still travel and still dream

Walking

Walking alone through the lonely old streets

just me, then a cat that my solitude meets

A pat and a snuggle

a start, a retreat

an owl in the darkness

and a breeze through light sleet

A dark quiet village at the base of a hill

where I wandered while young

and I wander now, still

The Struggle

Why do we agonize

over things that no longer exist?

Days that are done and people who are gone?

Why do we worry

about things that may never come?

Seeking the dark rather than enjoying brief sun?

There just is today, and today and today...

No tomorrow will arrive, no return to yesterday

Today and today and today and today...

Why do we struggle to live life that way?

Being an adult

Being an adult
is largely about pretending
that you have grown up
disguising the inner child
with words and bluster
and serious demeanor
while inside still wandering
the roads of fantasy and nonsense
that you used to travel openly
but now making sure that nobody notices
until back home alone
in the darkness
the child returns
to laugh
and cry
inside

I do remember

I do remember
some first coming into consciousness
with a glimmer of
'Oh... what's this here?'
but in pure thought
rather than unlearned words
while lying on a bed
looking out of a very young head
that became this much older one
now wondering about being dead
and still pondering
but now with some fear
'Oh... what's this here?'

That Cloud Again

Yes. It has been here before
The one inside my head
'It can just be personality,' a doctor said
While elaborating on my thoughts
I tended to agree
'Your thoughts are true
but best not dwelt upon,' said she
'Turn away from reality?
Is that what you suggest?'
'Sometimes,' she said
'That's for the best.'
adding, 'Look at me, and what I see?'
Which prompted me to offer
that she was much like me
'Perhaps,' she said
'But I prefer not to say.'
And we smiled
and wished each other 'Good Day.'

Gone

A pattern of thoughts
in a head much like mine
was extinguished last night
at too early a time
A fine person has gone
I think not anywhere
just dissipated and vanished
as into thin air
Others may tell me
to hope for his soul
but my sad contemplation
sees a dark empty hole
For what had a beginning
must too have an end
Not that I know, though
but goodbye my friend

Gone, dammit

Guilt, uselessness, inadequacy
pointlessness wondering why
Anger, hurt and annoyance
looking upwards to see only sky
Another one taken the option
that comes at the end of despair
one evening talking quite sensibly
the next morning no longer there
Hidden mostly by bluster
occasional wounds showing through
never revealing sufficient
until goodbye forever to you

Buildings and Birds

Big buildings built from heavy stones
raised high towards the sky
prove life as much as any bird
that flapping flutters by
All improbable constructions
doomed to crumble or to die

Bloomin' Birthday Boy... Bah...

Fifty-eight circles
around the sun are done
so here we bloomin' go now
on another bloomin' one
I did not ask to take this ride
in life I had no say
just 'here you are' and 'on you go'
and 'do it', day by day
So round and round and round and round
and round and round I spun
sometimes feeling all was lost
and sometimes that I'd won
on fifty-eight bloomin' circles
round a hot and shining sun

But...

I didn't ask my children

if they'd like this journey too

I just eyed up my lady and thought

Oh I fancy you

And thus does bloomin' nature

keep the carousel so busy

with unasked puzzled riders

spinning round and round 'til dizzy

Fine

A place to write rubbish

a tree to see

and all is fine

for a while with me

Sunday School

Here are gathered boys and girls
and fresh-faced adults too
to tell them to believe in things
they cannot know are true
The atmosphere is innocent
the people seeming nice
but then proceeds abuse of minds
by subtle faith's device
Abused become abusers
as the sinister cycle turns
the brain-washed become brain-washers
and the nonsense onward runs

Stop Thinking

Just stopping thinking is the thing to do
when thinking starts to trouble you
when depression looms and worries gather
and thinking gets you in a lather
Stop
Desist
Just cease for now
the churning mind and furrowed brow
just wait and face the present only
You will feel better, soon or slowly

Anxiety burns

Anxiety burns
like a fire in a head
consuming activity
and trapping in bed
Just getting up
is a step that is tough
but just getting up
is often enough

CalMac and Me

I would much rather be on a CalMac ferry

heading out on a glittering sea

feeling the wind and watching the headlands

shifting and flowing in mist around me

with gulls circling hopefully, looking for chips

the sound of the engines, that rhythm of ships

the gentlest of heaving in a moderate swell

the old ferry feeling that all is now well

It passes

It passes

it passes

(and then it returns)

The sadness and madness

anxiety burns

The stress and the mess

swilling inside a head

The thought that the next rhyme

is better not said

It passes

it passes

(and then will return)

but it passes, it passes

Remember the sun

Onward

From this moment on
in the bubble of now
only the future
can be cut by my plough
The past was all furrowed
and blurrowed and messed
but I'll just blunder on now
and try for the best

Bubbles of Then

Bubbles of Then
all gone, again
The practice of Zen
and the powers of ten
The factors of zero
the fiddling of Nero
The heart of a coward
enclosing a hero?
Meaningless words
or a secret within?
The bubbles are rising
as the new ones begin

I want to hear seagulls

I want to hear seagulls
and the wash of the sea
with the warmth of the sun
on the face outside me
as the sounds and the feelings
touch the mind deep within
letting return of contentment begin

To live like a cat

To live like a cat
knowing only the Now
accepting a pat
with a purr
Catching a bird
with a glance of the eye
and thinking of nothing
but stopping it fly
or stretched in the sun
with the warmth soaking in
unaware of the past
or the days yet to run
Just to live like a cat
knowing only the Now
accepting a pat
with a purr

Inheritance

Ignore the past
begin the future
inheriting what's given
from this day on
making further progress
as made beforehand
Enjoy what's here
forget what's gone

Delusion Illusion

The power of delusion

is the strongest we've got

believing in things

that simply are not

Convincing a mind

to change without aid

dreaming a dream

then finding it made

Delusion illusion

where nothing is real

except the fine feeling

that delusioners feel

The Force

The Placebo

The Gods

The Power

That sees what's real and while laughing, devours

Our Star

Hydrogen to Helium
that is all
in a big and brilliant ball
Simple
bright
our heat
our light
all that stops the endless night
Ever-changing
a different sun
than what was there
when I was young
Going, going, going
gone
Coming, coming
the end of dawn

To be

How the hell would I know
what is going on?
I'm merely made of atoms
singing their own song
or maybe something deeper
but nothing known to me
my place is just to ponder
and simply briefly be

Not today

When the time comes
but the time is not now
When the time comes
it will be dealt with
but how?
When the time comes
I will find a way
but it is not time
not that time today

Slam down the shutters

Seal yourself off
from the past and the future
slam down the bright shutters
with mirror effect
Look into the moment
and get on with living
accepting what happened
and forgetting what's done
The bubble, the bubble
the bubble of Now
again and again stay in it
somehow
Then lift that front shutter whenever you dare
looking forward to see what's offered out there
but keep the other one slammed tight shut
don't ever look back
no 'if' and no 'but'

In the forest of the mind

Walking every day in the forest of the mind
and if sinking in mud
having the sense to turn back
thinking
'Oh. I don't like this track'
You can pull your thoughts out
and onto a sunnier way
for the forest offers everything
but your thoughts can seize the day
Avoid those dark wanderings
and seek out the sun
Navigation is not easy
but it still can be done
Everything is in there
but care is required
just avoid the thorny thickets
and find what's desired

Just do

If a day seems meaningless
you have to give it meaning
by finding something to do
that can become meaningful to you
Easy to say, not often easy to do
But better than being miserable
just doing something slowly
just try to do

Changing everything

When you cannot change a thing
you can still change your attitude to all things

"Everything can be taken from a man or a woman but one thing: the last of human freedoms - to choose one's attitude in any given set of circumstances..." Viktor Frankl

When you cannot change a thing
you can still change your attitude to all things

and in doing so
you can change everything

Pythagoras Wake

In mathematics

see everything

the waves in bits

and bits in waves

Each temporary foaming too

a metaphor of me and you

The situation given

The situation given
is the place you should begin
as if just born this instant
at some greater being's whim
For every day you waken
a consciousness begins
to last one day then ending
as the day's light slowly dims

An obvious choice

So what are you going to do

when you feel so bad?

Lie in misery and bleat?

Admit defeat?

Or get up and on with something

to slowly beat

the damn depression off

the fog away

and make something better

out of what began as a miserable day?

Rest, if needed is fine

Dwelling in gloom is bad

Get up

move on

and slowly lose the sad…

…says I, the man, the husband, dad

the one remembering the hopeful lad

Too late?

How did I get old?
By doing nothing
I'm told
Just letting time pass
and not getting on
missing my chances
fluffing the song
Starting again now
Left it too late?
Just give it a go
Don't sit
Don't wait

Epilogue

The closest thing I have ever had to the feeling of an epiphany came when I looked into the eyes of a friend and suddenly the thought just came to me that it was like looking in a mirror.

It seemed, in that instant, on that long lost evening, that I suddenly realized my connection to the sea of consciousness and that perhaps we are all just brief upwellings of the same damn thing.

And if, for a moment, we could feel what it was like to be another person, that we might just think, 'Oh... It's still me!'

You see?
Just frothy waves
in the conscious sea
Maybe
Identity, all blurry
you, and them
and me

Also by Andrew MacLaren-Scott

Aileen the Alien

Alien Island

Report on Sample 717

After The Lady Lord

and writing as Andrew Scott

Life's Science – the prose poems

andrewmaclarenscott.blogspot.co.uk